The level of violence perpetrated by or on behalf of Mexican drug cartels[1] has reached unprecedented levels, especially in northern Mexico. Since 2007, nearly 40,000 people have been murdered in cartel-related violence. Most violence takes place among the cartels, but attacks on the security forces have increased since President Calderon began targeting the DTOs in 2007. Associated crimes such as murder for hire, money laundering, kidnapping, extortion, and human trafficking follow in the wake of the drug trade. Pockets of northern Mexico lie outside of government control, while the *estado* of Tamaulipas is arguably becoming a failed state within Mexico.[2] Judging by homicide statistics alone, neighboring Chihuahua is even worse off. American citizens on both sides of the border are increasingly among the victims of cartel violence.

A number of scholars look at the mayhem in northern Mexico and see an insurgency. Often they use the term as a prelude to advocating a counterinsurgency-based approach to the drug cartels. Much of this analysis, however, appears to be an attempt to redefine what constitutes an insurgency in order to apply the "lessons" of COIN to Mexico. Try as they might, many of these observers cannot escape the perception that they are trying to define a problem that will fit their solution.

Mexico, however, is not a failed state. Those who argue that poverty and deprivation are the root of Mexico's problems ignore the fact that Mexico is a middle-income country with a *per capita* GDP 25 times higher than that of Afghanistan and more

---

[1] This paper will use the terms drug cartel, DTO (drug-trafficking organization) and TCO (transnational criminal organization) interchangeably when referring to Mexican drug-trafficking organizations.

[2] Gary J. Hale, "A 'Failed State' in Mexico: Tamaulipas Declares Itself Ungovernable," James A. Baker Institute for Public Policy, Rice University (2011).

than five times that of Iraq.[3] Prior to the current economic downturn, 60 percent of the population was considered middle class.[4] Mexico has had a stable – if not entirely democratic -- political system since the early 1930s. Its Institutional Revolutionary Party (PRI), for all its faults, presided over a relatively benign variety of one-party rule characterized by broad political mobilization, institution-building and economic development.[5] Unlike most Latin American countries, post-revolutionary Mexico has no history of military rule. With the election of President Vicente Fox in 2000, 70 years of one-party rule by the PRI came to an end. While the homicide rate in northern Mexico is appalling, the country as a whole has a murder rate lower than many Central American and Caribbean countries.[6] Taken together, the four most violent states in northern Mexico have a combined murder rate similar to that of Honduras.[7] And despite increasing violence, the 2010 state and local elections saw Mexicans rejecting candidates perceived to be backed by the cartels.[8] Mexico, it seems, is not as bad off as it is sometimes portrayed.

This paper will argue that Mexican drug cartels and associated criminal groups do *not* constitute an insurgency. It would therefore be counterproductive for the United

---

[3] World Bank, "GDP per capita (current U.S. $)," http://data.worldbank.org/indicator/NY.GDP.PCAP.CD

[4] Jorge Castañeda, "Mexico's Failed Drug War," Cato Institute Economic Development Bulletin, No. 13 (6 May 2010).

[5] See, for example, the sections on Mexico in Samuel P. Huntington's classic Political Order in Changing Societies; or, for a more readable journalistic account, Alan Riding's Distant Neighbors: A Portrait of the Mexicans.

[6] United Nations Office on Drugs and Crime (UNODC), "Global Study on Homicide 2011. http://www.unodc.org/documents/data-and-analysis/statistics/Homicide/Globa_study_on_homicide_2011_web.pdf

[7] Ibid.

[8] Marc Lacy, "Mexican Democracy, Even Under Seige,," New York Times, July 5, 2010. file:///Users/bradfreden/Desktop/JMO%20Mexico%20Paper/Even%20Under%20Siege,%20Mexico's%20Democracy%20Endures%20-%20NYTimes.com.webarchive

States or Mexico to adopt a COIN strategy toward the interrelated problems of drug trafficking, violence and lawlessness in Mexico, as some have argued.

The first section below will examine the claims that the Mexican cartels constitute an insurgency. The second will examine the shortcomings and risks of applying a population-centric COIN strategy to what is essentially a law-enforcement problem in Mexico. The final section will highlight elements of COIN *a la carte* that are or should be part of our current approach.

I. Is Mexico Facing an Insurgency?

As the wars in Afghanistan and Iraq approach the ten-year mark, discussion of insurgency and counterinsurgency among Americans has gone viral. No longer are these topics the exclusive domain of Army outcasts wearing green berets or obscure civilian strategists on the fringes of academia. COIN, in particular, has entered the popular lexicon since the success of the "surge" in Iraq and President Obama's embrace of the Petraeus/McChrystal brand of counterinsurgency in Afghanistan. Everyone, it seems, has been influenced by what Douglas Lovelace, Jr., the Director of the Strategic Studies Institute at the Army War College calls "the COIN fever of our time."[9] The Kindle version of the U.S. Army <u>Counterinsurgency Field Manual</u> (FM 3-24) is currently #12 on Amazon.com's list of best sellers in military strategy, just four places behind Tom Clancy's <u>Carrier</u>.[10] According to <u>Foreign Affairs</u> magazine, the COIN FM "has helped

---

[9] Douglass Lovelace, Jr., in the forward to "David Galula: His Life and Intellectual Context," by Ann Marlowe. Carlisle, PA: Strategic Studies Institute (August 2010).
[10] www.amazon.com, accessed by the author on 7 October 2011.

make counterinsurgency part of the zeitgeist."[11] The manual "has become a coffee-table staple in Washington," even leading to the appearance of one of its drafters, LTC John Nagl, on The Daily Show with Jon Stewart. Given all this hype, is it any wonder that COIN is beginning to be seen as the cure-all for a host of international ills?

Before COIN can be applied to Mexico, however, there needs to be an insurgency. The "narco-insurgency" paradigm, increasingly common in the literature on Mexican drug cartels, is the route chosen by many advocates of COIN. Among the scholarly proponents of insurgency in Mexico is Robert Bunker, who argues that "criminal and spiritual insurgencies are now taking place in Mexico," and foresees these groups attaining "*de facto* political control" if current trends persist.[12] Diana Villiers Negroponte, writing for the Brookings Institute, skips over the issue of whether the DTOs constitute an insurgency, but asserts that the cartels "are more powerful than the government" and argues for counterinsurgency in response.[13] Levant Kiran, writing for the Project on International Security at the College of William and Mary, says Mexico faces a "narco-commercialist insurgency" that seeks to "control territory for economic rather than traditional political reasons."[14] Nevertheless, he rejects COIN in favor of a more-or-less traditional law enforcement strategy. On the military side, Major Terry Hilderbrand, writing at the U.S. Army Command and Staff College in 2011, makes a detailed argument that Mexico is facing a "narco-insurgency," quoting in support the assertion

[11] Colin H Kahl., "COIN of the Realm: Is There a Future for Counterinsurgency?" Foreign Affairs, November/December 2007.

[12] Dr. Robert J. Bunker, "Criminal (Cartel & Gang) Insurgencies in Mexico and the Americas: What you need to know, not what you want to hear." Testimony Before the House Foreign Affairs Committee Subcommittee on Western Hemisphere Affairs (13 September 2011).

[13] Diana Villiers Negroponte, "Mexico Denies 'Insurgency': Implications for an Appropriate Response," Brookings Institution (27 October 2010).

[14] Levant Kiran, "A Different Fight: Narco-Commercialist Insurgencies in Mexico." Project on International Peace and Security, The College of William and Mary (2010).

that Mexico is facing "violent imposition of radical socioeconomic restructuring of the state and its governance in accordance with criminal values."[15] LCDR David Deuel compares the seven major Mexican cartels to "the numerous tribes and clans in Afghanistan;" he then goes on to advocate FM 3-24's model of "Clear, Hold and Build" for Mexico.[16] All of these analyses have one thing in common: an attempt to pound the square peg of criminal violence into the round hole of insurgency.

Political leaders, such as Congressman Connie Mack (R-FL), Chairman of the Western Hemisphere Subcommittee of the HFAC, use the term "insurgency" to criticize current policy and call for a more robust, whole-of-government approach to the cartels.[17] Even Secretary of State Hillary Clinton used the "I-word" in her September 2010 remarks to the Council on Foreign Relations,[18] angering Mexican officials and prompting a rare public correction by the President.

Among policymakers and scholars alike, the term "insurgency" is sometimes used as synonym for organized violence by a non-state actor. Insurgency is a useful metaphor because it captures the urgency of the situation, the violence and the threat to the authority of the state. It is not, however, an accurate description of what is happening in Mexico. One need look no further than the above-mentioned Counterinsurgency Field Manual, FM 3-24, to find the characteristics of an insurgency:

---

[15] MAJ Terry Neil Hildebrand, Jr., "Drug Trafficking Within Mexico: A Law-Enforcement Issue or Insurgency?" Masters thesis, U.S. Army Command and General Staff College (2011), p. 88.
[16] LCDR David S. Deuel, "Drug Cartels and Gangs in Central America: A View Through the Lens of Counterinsurgency," Masters thesis, Joint Forces Staff College, Norfolk, VA (2010). Like some other writers, Deuel mistakenly asserts that COIN brought down the Colombian drug cartels, when in fact it was only applied to the FARC, not the cartels (see below).
[17] Hon. Connie Mack (R-FL), Chairman, Western Hemisphere Subcommittee, House Foreign Affairs Committee; opening statement for hearing entitled, "Has Mérida Evolved? Part One: The Evolution of Drug Cartels and the Threat to Mexico's Governance," 13 September 2011.
[18] Hillary Rodham Clinton, Secretary of State, Remarks to the Council on Foreign Relations, Washington, DC, 8 September 2010.

Joint doctrine defines an insurgency as an organized movement aimed at the overthrow of a constituted government through the use of subversion and armed conflict (JP 1-02). Stated another way, an insurgency is an organized, protracted political-military struggle designed to weaken the control and legitimacy of an established government, occupying power, or other political authority, while increasing insurgent control. . . . In all cases, insurgents aim to force political change; any military action is secondary and subordinate.[19]

According to Bard O'Neill, one of the foremost contemporary experts on

insurgency and counterinsurgency,

Insurgency may be defined as a struggle between a nonruling group and the ruling authorities in which the nonruling group consciously uses *political resources* (e.g., organizational expertise, propaganda, and demonstrations) and *violence* to destroy reformulate or sustain the basis of legitimacy . . . . (emphasis in the original.)[20]

David Kilcullen, the author of the "Three Pillars" approach to COIN, appears to agree:

An insurgency is a struggle for control over a contested *political* space, between a state (or group of states or occupying powers) and one or more *popularly-based* non-state challengers. *Insurgencies are popular uprisings* that grow from, and are conducted through pre-existing social networks . . . . (Emphasis added.)[21]

In short, the cartels may be an uber-violent mafia, but they are not an insurgency by any

stretch of the imagination. Their goal is profit, not power. They neither have nor seek to

acquire broad-based popular support. To do so would require a marketable belief system,

whether sincere or merely cynical, to put their violence in political context and attract (or

indoctrinate) followers.

---

[19] U.S. Army Field Manual 3-24: Counterinsurgency. Washington, DC: Department of the Army (15 December 2006).

[20] Bard O'Neill, Insurgency and Terrorism: From Revolution to Apocalypse, 2nd edition. Potomac Books, Inc., 2005.

[21] David J. Kilcullen, "Three Pillars of Counterinsurgency," remarks delivered to the U.S. Government Counterinsurgency Conference in Washington, DC 28 September 2006.
http://www.au.af.mil/au/awc/awcgate/uscoin/3pillars_of_counterinsurgency.pdf

Ideology --whether political, religious or ethnic -- is a defining characteristic of insurgency that is conspicuously lacking from the cartels. According to Steven Metz and Raymond Millen,

> National insurgencies in particular depend on ideology to unify, inspire, [and] explain why the existing system is unjust or illegitimate, and rationalize the use of violence to alter or overthrow the existing system.[22]

The closest scholars have come to identifying a political agenda behind the cartel activity is to posit that they seek to weaken or co-opt local, state, and, to a lesser extent, federal governments in Mexico in order to be able to conduct their criminal activities unhindered. This is the cornerstone of the "narco-insurgency" argument cited above. Whether it is true or simply a truism that the cartels seek to weaken the ability and the will of the Mexican government to enforce the law, this does not amount to an ideology or even a coherent political agenda. The cartels make no effort to convince the masses that weakening the government or allowing the cartels free reign is a good idea (which would be a tough sell in any society), nor to usurp the functions of government. Like Al Capone and Pablo Escobar, Mexican cartel leaders feed their egos and protect their flanks by lavishing charity on their hometowns or bases of operation, but this largesse is not able or intended to usurp the role of government. To the extent that the cartels are pursuing a political agenda, it is simply to be left alone by law enforcement. This is 1920's Chicago on steroids, not Afghanistan, Iraq or even Colombia.

Some scholars point to the religious mysticism of the *La Familia Michoacána* or *Los Caballeros Templarios* (The Knights of Templar) arguing that, like the Taliban, they

---

[22] Steven Metz and Raymond Millen, "Insurgency and Counterinsurgency in the 21st century: Reconceptualizing Threat and Response," p. 6. Carlisle, PA: U.S. Army Strategic Studies Institute, 2004.

are motivated at least in part by religious fervor.[23] However, fervent belief in the power

of religious icons and patron saints is a staple of Mexican folk religion and has been for

centuries. This cult-like devotion to certain saints, common to varying degrees

throughout Latin America, is no more the ideology of Mexican drug traffickers than it is

of Mexican bus drivers, who ostentatiously glorify similar religious icons. Dangerous

occupations, not drug trafficking, are the tie that binds, as anyone who has ever ridden a

bus in Mexico will attest. Mexican cartel members are no more fighting for *Santa*

Muerte than Mexican bus drivers are speeding for the Virgin Mary. Religious beliefs,

rituals and even sacrifices are a form of protection, not a *casus belli*.[24]

Proponents of criminal insurgency, narco-insurgency, "narco-commercialist

insurgency,"[25] and other hyphenated insurgencies argue that traditional concepts are

outdated. Since its inception, however, the concept of insurgency has been predicated on

a "Clausewitzian" understanding of the insurgents' motivation (even before Clausewitz,

if that makes sense). Whether their cause was ideological, ethnic or religious, violence

has always been "the continuation of politics by different means." In other words, the

object of insurgency is political power: seizing it or changing the manner in which it is

exercised. The political objective is an end unto itself. What delineates the cartels from

insurgents is that they see political influence as a *means*, not an end. DTOs exist to make

---

[23] See, for example, Dr Robert Bunker's lurid testimony before the House Foreign Affairs Committee on Western Hemisphere Affairs on 13 September 2011 or, less sensationally, Iaon Grillo, "Drug-Dealing for Jesus: Mexico's Evangelical Narcos." Time, 19 July 2009.

[24] "'Saint Death' comes to Chicago," Chicago Tribune, 30 September 2007. Though it goes beyond the scope of this paper, anthropologists have pointed out the manner in which the practice of the Roman Catholic faith in the Americas has been influenced by pre-Colombian culture, including death cults. *Dia de Los Muertos* ("Day of the Dead"), a macabre version of All Saints' Day celebrated throughout Mexico on November 1, is one of its modern-day manifestations.

[25] Levant Kiran, "A Different Fight: Narco-Commercialist Insurgencies in Mexico," Policy Briefs 2009-2010, pp. 17-26. The College of William and Mary: Project on International Peace and Security (2010). http://irtheoryandpractice.wm.edu/projects/PIPS/PIPS.2009-2010.PolicyBriefBook.pdf

money; any political aspirations they might have are distinctly subordinate. This may seem like a distinction without a difference, but it has important implications for understanding and combating the cartels.

II. So What?

The reader could be forgiven for asking whether this is just a theological argument about the nature of insurgency. It is not. Defining Mexico's interrelated problems of violence, drug trafficking and lawlessness as an insurgency is not only intellectually flawed, it leads to the mistaken conclusion that COIN should be the response. However, for political as well as practical reasons, COIN is the wrong approach to Mexico's current problems. In the absence of an actual insurgency, COIN will, at best, lead Mexico and the United States squander their resources by applying them to ineffectual and unnecessary efforts to "win over" the Mexican population. Moreover, as we have seen, the term "insurgency" is anathema to the Mexican government; for Washington to embrace COIN as the solution to Mexico's problems would be politically counterproductive, to put it mildly.

A population-centric COIN approach to the DTOs –- isolating the population from the "insurgents" and winning them over to the government's cause -- would be a classic example of misdirected effort. Similarly, repackaging traditional development assistance as counterinsurgency, which COIN advocates seem to want to do in Mexico's case, is not helpful because it creates a perception that the United States is looking at

Mexico through the lens of its recent experience in Afghanistan and Iraq.[26] This plays into Mexico's historical neuralgia about U.S. military intervention.

Some who argue for a COIN strategy in Mexico make explicit reference to the "Clear, Hold and Build" approach applied with varying degrees of success in Iraq and Afghanistan.[27] Others draw on Colombia's experience, the writings of French COIN expert David Galula or the "Three Pillars" approach of Dr. David Kilcullen. While each of these approaches has merit in other contexts, all suffer from the same defect when applied to Mexico: they are, to a greater or lesser extent, focused on controlling and/or winning over the population. The problem in Mexico, however, is not the population. When it comes to fighting the cartels and reestablishing the rule of law in areas of cartel dominance, the overwhelming majority of Mexicans already support the government. According to a recent Global Attitudes poll by the respected Pew Research Center, the vast majority of Mexicans see crime (80%) or drug-cartel violence (77%) as their country's number-one problem. Even larger numbers support the Calderon government's aggressive efforts against the cartels, with 84% favoring the use of the military against DTOs.[28]

Fear, the other motivating factor employed by the cartels, cannot compel long-term support; at best, it can only enforce neutrality.[29] Moreover, when it comes to

---

[26] At least since the author joined the Foreign Service 21 years ago, USAID and the Department of State have been helping countries fight poverty, implement sustainable economic-growth policies, develop effective law-enforcement and judicial systems, and strengthen civil society, all outside the rubric of COIN.

[27] See for example Hillderbrand and Deuel.

[28] Pew Research Center, "Crime and Drug Cartels Top Concerns in Mexico;" Global Attitudes Project, 31 August 2011.

[29] The exceptions – e.g., kidnapped Central American migrants forced at gunpoint to do the cartels' bidding -- are sufficiently rare as to prove the rule. This type of support is brittle, to put it mildly, and

indiscriminate violence, cartels are subject to the same laws of political physics as governments: harsh treatment, human rights violations and atrocities create more enemies than they eliminate. In a situation where the absence of a coherent ideology limits the appeal of the cartels to those who benefit directly, the Counterinsurgency Field Manual has limited relevance. The enemy, in the form of the cartels and their paid enablers, is the sole target.

Moreover, despite protests that COIN is primarily a non-military activity, there are few examples of successful counterinsurgency that did not rely to a significant extent on the deployment of military forces in a combat role. For this reason, democracies are understandably cautious about employing a COIN strategy against a domestic criminal threat. This is largely uncharted territory, Colombia's experience notwithstanding, and governments such as Mexico's can be forgiven for approaching it with caution.

Among COIN advocates, comparisons with Colombia are many, but the actual parallels with Mexico are few. The FARC morphed into a true narco-insurgency, but, unlike the Mexican cartels, it started off as a Marxist-Leninist insurgency with an explicitly political agenda. Proponents of hyphenated insurgencies have yet to point to a criminal organization that evolved in the opposite direction, and their efforts to shoehorn Mexico into this role have so far proven unconvincing.

---

certainly turns far more average Mexicans against the cartels. Fear-induced passivity on the part of local populations is, however, an undeniably important factor in the cartels' ability to operate unhindered by law enforcement.

The FARC and the Colombian cartels had a symbiotic relationship, but they are far from synonymous.[30] Nor were the FARC ever more than one player in Colombia's multi-faceted drug trade. Advocates of a COIN strategy in Mexico point to its relatively successful employment against the FARC, but COIN was never adopted as a strategy for fighting the notorious Cali and Medellin cartels, even when these cartels were waging a campaign of violent intimidation against the Colombian government much like the one we see in Mexico today. The Colombian cartels were effectively dealt with as a law enforcement problem, with the police in the lead, while the military dealt with the FARC using a COIN model.[31] Those who advocate applying the COIN lessons of Colombia to Mexico tend to gloss over this fact, conflating the FARC and the cartels. However, none of the oft-cited tenets of COIN -- population control, winning hearts and minds, rural and urban development programs –- were major factors in Colombia's success against the traditional drug cartels, which the Mexican DTOs resemble far more closely than they resemble the FARC.[32] Rather, success against the Colombian cartels resulted from taking down their leadership structure.

III. COIN *a la carte*

If we strip COIN of its military (at least in the minds of many people) overtones and its focus on controlling or winning over the population, are there aspects of COIN

---

[30] Rafael Pardo, former Colombian Foreign Minister, "Colombia's Two-Front War," Foreign Affairs, July/August 2000.

[31] Robert C. Bonner, "The New Cocaine Cowboys: How to Defeat Mexico's Drug Cartels," Foreign Affairs, July/August 2010.

[32] The Mexican cartels are not qualitatively different from the Cali and Medellin cartels in terms of their level of violence or their targeting of government officials. As former Colombian Foreign Minister Rafael Pardo points out above (Pardo, "Colombia's Two-Front War), the Medellin and Cali cartels murdered judges, police officers, journalists, and even presidential candidates seemingly at will.

that can usefully be applied to defeating Mexico's supercharged TCOs? The answer is yes, and many of them are already being applied as part of the current approach:

Law enforcement: Long before the Colombian government succeeded in fusing intelligence and law enforcement to defeat the infamous Cali and Medellin cartels, counterinsurgency experts were applying this model as part of a successful strategy to defeat uprisings in Malaya and elsewhere. In fact, the line between COIN and law enforcement is a blurry one. Just as organized crime and insurgency can be seen as different points on a broad spectrum of low-intensity conflict, police and military forces can be seen as part of a continuum of responses.

Military operations: In the short term at least, Mexican military forces will be required to fill the vacuum created by the breakdown of local and, to a lesser extent, federal law enforcement. This will require a reorientation and retraining of at least some units of the Mexican Army and Navy, away from territorial defense and toward robust domestic law enforcement. Aspects of U.S. COIN doctrine contained in FM 3-24, particularly the emphasis on positive interaction with the civilian population, avoidance of collateral damage and use of the minimum necessary force to accomplish the mission, are valuable in this regard.

Intelligence sharing: Accurate intelligence allows security forces – civilian or military – to find and arrest or kill the enemy while minimizing false arrests or civilian casualties, as the case may be. All-source U.S. intelligence was a major factor in Colombia's successful effort to turn the tide against both the FARC and the drug cartels.[33] The United States has reportedly helped Mexico create and run two intelligence "fusion cells" aimed at tracking down cartel leaders.[34] If Mexico is to succeed in bringing down the drug cartels, it will be, as in the case of Colombia, this fusion of intelligence and quick-strike, paramilitary capability that does it.

Whole-of-government approach: The United States has yet to get this right in Iraq and Afghanistan, but it has recognized the need and is moving in the right direction. In 2009, the State Department, with input from eight other agencies and departments, published the U.S. Government Counterinsurgency Guide.[35] While the Guide focuses primarily on defeating higher-order insurgencies rather than TCOs, its "whole-of-government" approach is an essential ingredient for meeting any serious security or foreign-policy challenge. Critics of the current, Merida Initiative approach to defeating the cartels, prominent among them Congressman Connie Mack (R-FL), call for precisely this whole-of-government approach: "An all US agency plan . . . to aggressively attack and dismantle the criminal networks in the United States and Mexico."[36] Few would disagree with this approach, or with the need to better-coordinate our efforts across bureaucratic and political lines.

"Emergency" extradition procedures: The Calderon government has sharply increased the number of criminal suspects extradited to the United States.[37] This is a

---

[33] Max Boot and Richard Bennet, "The Colombian Miracle: How Alvaro Uribe turned the tide against drug lords and Marxist Guerillas," The Weekly Standard, 14 December 2009. http://www.weeklystandard.com/Content/Public/Articles/000/000/017/301nyrut.asp?pg=1
[34] Mark Mazzetti and Ginger Thompson, "U.S. Widens Role in Mexican Fight," New York Times, 25 August 2011.
[35] United States Government Interagency Counterinsurgency Initiative, U.S. Government Counterinsurgency Guide. Washington, DC: U.S. Department of State (2009).
[36] Mack, "Has Merida Evolved?"
[37] Bonner, "Cocaine Cowboys."

welcome development not simply because it allows the United States to prosecute those accused of committing crimes that impact the United States or its citizens, but because it compensates for the current weakness of the Mexican criminal justice system by allowing certain accused criminals to be taken out of that system. Nevertheless, many accused cartel members are still able to avoid extradition by manipulating this same judicial system. The Calderon government should consider using existing emergency powers and/or new legislation to temporarily suspend some of the procedural impediments to rapid extradition, not to please the United States, but to deal a decisive blow to the cartels and restore order in its northern border states. Other democracies, including the UK, Spain and Italy have adopted temporary emergency measures to fight terrorism, insurgencies or organized crime. By temporarily suspending the right of previously-named individuals to appeal their extradition, Mexico would buy itself time as it reforms its own criminal justice system.[38]

IV. Conclusion: Rewriting the Bilateral Narrative

Historically, the U.S. approach to Mexico has swung between benign neglect and breathless alarm. When Mexico's problems spilled over our borders, we paid attention; when problems receded, Mexico became just another country struggling to get its calls returned by busy Washington policymakers. Mexico, meanwhile, regarded its northern neighbor with justifiable suspicion.[39] If Mexico is to be our partner in "the war on drugs"

---

[38] A court structured along the lines of the U.S. Foreign Intelligence Surveillance Court (FISC) could review and pre-approve extradition of select, high-value cartel leaders or, at a minimum, hold expedited, closed-door extradition hearings for any previously-identified individual brought before the court. In order to comply with the Mexican constitution, the U.S. would have to agree in advance not to seek the death penalty for these individuals.

[39] See, for example, Riding's <u>Distant Neighbors</u> or Castañeda and Robert A. Pastor, <u>Limits to Friendship: The United States and Mexico.</u>

and other important international endeavors, the bilateral paradigm must be updated. We must demonstrate by our actions that we see Mexico as an equal partner in a bilateral relationship built on trust and better understanding of each other's societies. Whether recently-minted terms like criminal insurgency, narco-insurgency and even narco-commercialist insurgency add value or understanding to these efforts is questionable. One could be forgiven for seeing them instead as just another round of alarmist hyperventilation brought on in part by the contemporary obsession with COIN.

One thing, however, seems clear: given the still-speculative nature of the narco-insurgency paradigm, neither we nor the Mexican government should be too quick to rush down the path of counterinsurgency, simply (or even partially) because it has become fashionable in recent years. With the exception of Canada, no country is more important to our core national security than Mexico. We cannot afford to get it wrong, or to confuse the operational objective of defeating the drug cartels with strategic objective of ensuring a friendly, prosperous, secure, and democratic neighbor to the south.

Bibliography

Anderson, Martin Edwin. "A Roadmap for Beating Latin America's Transnational Criminal Organizations." Joint Forces Quarterly, Issue 62, 3rd quarter 2011, pp. 81-88.

Bahney, Benjamin, Jack K. Reiley and Agnes G. Schaefer. "Security in Mexico: Implications for U.S. Policy Options." Santa Monica, CA: RAND (2009).

Baker, Biff. "The United State and Mexico Enhanced Military Cooperation." DISAM Journal of International Security Assistance Management 29, no. 3 (July 2009).

Baker, Biff, and Victor E. Renuart. "U.S.-Mexico Homeland Defense: A Compatible Interface." Institute for National Strategic Studies no. 254. Washington, DC: National Defense University (October 2010).

Bonner, Robert C. "The New Cocaine Cowboys: How to Defeat Mexico's Drug Cartels." Foreign Affairs, July/August 2010.

Boot, Max and Richard Bennet. "How Alvaro Uribe with Smart U.S. support turned the tide against drug lords and Marxist Guerillas." The Weekly Standard, 14 December 2009. http://www.weeklystandard.com/Content/Public/Articles/000/000/017/301nyrut.asp?pg=1

Bunker, Dr. Robert J. "Criminal (Cartel & Gang) Insurgencies in Mexico an the Americas: What you need to know, not what you want to hear." Testimony Before the House Foreign Affairs Committee Subcommittee on Western Hemisphere Affairs (13 September 2011).

Callafono, Dr. James Jay, et al. "Expand NORAD to Improve Security in North America," Heritage Foundation Backgrounder, 27 July 2010.

Camp, Roderic Ai. "Armed Forces and Drugs: Public Perceptions and Institutional Challenges," in Eric L. Olson, David A. Shirk, and Andrew Selee, eds., Shared Responsibility: U.S.-Mexico Policy Options for Confronting Organized Crime (Washington, D.C.: Woodrow Wilson Center for Scholars and the University of San Diego, 2010), 291-326.

Castañeda, Jorge. "Mexico's Failed Drug War." Cato Institute Economic Development Bulletin, No. 13, 6 May 2010. http://www.cato.org/pub_display.php?pub_id=11746

_____ and Robert A. Pastor. Limits to Friendship: The United States and Mexico (Vintage: 1989).

Clinton, Hillary Rodham Clinton, U.S. Secretary of State. Remarks to the Council on

Foreign Relations in Washington, DC, 8 September 2010. http://www.cfr.org/us-strategy-and-politics/conversation-us-secretary-state-hillary-rodham-clinton-video/p22894

Corcoran, Patrick. "COIN in Mexico? A Response to Robert Culp's Strategy for Military Counter Drug Operations." Small Wars Journal, 5 March 2011.

Culp, Robert. "Strategy for Military Counterdrug Operations." Small Wars Journal, 24 January 2011.

Deuel, David S. "Drug Cartels and Gangs in Central America: A View Through the Lens of Counterinsurgency." Masters thesis, Joint Forces Staff College, Norfolk, VA (2010). DTIC: http://oai.dtic.mil/oai/oai?verb=getRecord&metadataPrefix=html&identifier=ADA530241

Fimiani, MAJ Clay T. "U.S. Northern Command's Security Role in Mexico: An Indirect Approach to Building Capacity Among the Mexican Military;." Joint Military Operations Department, U.S. Naval War College (May 2011).

Fischer, Max; "Why Drug Cartels are Mexico's Insurgency." The Atlantic (16 March 2010). http://www.theatlantic.com/international/archive/2010/03/why-drug-cartels-are-mexicos-insurgency/37573/

Galula, David, *Counterinsurgency Warfare: Theory and Practice*. Westport, Connecticut: Praeger Security International (1964).

Greene, Thomas H, Comparative Revolutionary Movements: Search for Theory and Justice. Englewood Cliffs, NJ: Prentice Hall (1984).

Grillo, Ioan, Author Q & A. http://ioangrillo.com/authorqa.php, accessed by the author on 10 October 2011.

_____. "Drug-Dealing for Jesus: Mexico's Evangelical Narcos." Time, 19 July 2009. http://www.time.com/time/world/article/0,8599,1911556,00.html

Guevara Moyano, Inigo. "Adapting, Transforming and Modernizing Under Fire: The Mexican Military 2006-11." Strategic Studies Institute, U.S. Army War College (September 2011).

Gurr, Ted Robert. Why Men Rebel. Princeton, NJ: Princeton University Press (1970).

Hale, Gary J. "A 'Failed State' in Mexico: Tamaulipas Declares Itself Ungovernable." James a Baker Institute for Public Policy, Rice University (2011).

Hildebrand, Jr., MAJ Terry Neil. "Drug Trafficking Within Mexico: A Law-Enforcement Issue or Insurgency?" Masters thesis, U.S. Army Command and

General Staff College (2011). Homeland Security Data Base
http://www.hsdl.org/?view&did=683118

Huntington, Samuel P. Political Order in Changing Societies. New Haven: Yale
University Press (1966).

Kahl, Colin H. "COIN of the Realm: Is There a Future for Counterinsurgency?"
Foreign Affairs, November/December 2007.

Kiran, Levant. "A Different Fight: Narco-Commercialist Insurgencies in Mexico.",
Policy Briefs 2009-2010, pp. 17-26. The College of William and Mary: Project
on International Peace and Security (2010).
http://irtheoryandpractice.wm.edu/projects/PIPS/PIPS.2009-
2010.PolicyBriefBook.pdf

Kilcullen, David J. "Three Pillars of Counterinsurgency." Remarks delivered to the U.S.
Government Counterinsurgency Conference. Washington, DC, 28 September
2006.
http://www.au.af.mil/au/awc/awcgate/uscoin/3pillars_of_counterinsurgency.pdf

Lacy, Marc. "Mexican Democracy, Even Under Siege." New York Times, July 5, 2010.
file:///Users/bradfreden/Desktop/JMO%20Mexico%20Paper/Even%20Under%20
Siege,%20Mexico's%20Democracy%20Endures%20-
%20NYTimes.com.webarchive

Mack, Hon. Connie; Chairman of the HFAC Western Hemisphere Subcommittee. "Has
Merida Evolved? Part One: The Evolution of Drug Cartels and the Threat to
Mexico's Governance." Statement to the Subcommittee. U.S. House of
Representatives (13 September 2011).

Marlowe, Ann. "David Galula: His Life and Intellectual Context," Carlyle, PA:
Strategic Studies Institute (August 2010).

Miller, LCDR Zachary J. "Counterinsurgency and the Mexican Drug War." Joint
Military Operations Department, U.S. Naval War College (2010).

Mullen, ADM Mike, CJCS. "Remarks at the Mexican Naval War College" (6 MAR
2009). http://www.jcs.mil/speech.aspx?ID=1141

Olson, Eric L. and Christopher E. Wilson. "Beyond Merida: The Evolving Approach to
Security Cooperation." Woodrow Wilson International Center for Scholars:
Trans-border Institute (May 2010).

O'Neill, Bard. Insurgency and Terrorism: From Revolution to Apocalypse, 2nd edition.
Potomac Books, Inc. (2005).

Pardo, Rafael. "Colombia's Two-Front War." Foreign Affairs, July/August 2000.

Pew Research Center. "Crime and Drug Cartels Top Concerns in Mexico." Global Attitudes Project, 31 August 2011.

Ribando Seelke, Claire, and Kristin M. Finklea. "U.S.-Mexico Security Cooperation: The Merida Initiative and Beyond." Congressional Research Service (31 JAN 2011).

Riding, Alan. Distant Neighbors: A Portrait of the Mexicans. New York: Vintage Books (1989).

Spinetta, Major Lawrence A., USAF. "Expanding North American Aerospace Defense: A Strategy to Engage Mexico." Air and Space Power, June 2005. http://www.airpower.au.af.mil/apjinternational/apj-s/2005/2tri05/spinettaeng.html

Sullivan, John P. and Adam Elkus. "State of Seige: Mexico's Criminal Insurgency." Small Wars Journal (2008). http://smallwarsjournal.com/jrnl/art/state-of-siege-mexicos-criminal-insurgency

Turbiville, Jr., Graham H. "U.S. Military Engagement with Mexico: Uneasy Past and Challenging Future" JSOU Report 10-2. Joint Special Operations University (March 2010).

United Nations Office on Drugs and Crime. "Global Study on Homicide: Trends, Contexts and Data." UNODC: 2011.

U.S. Army. Field Manual 3-24: Counterinsurgency. Washington, DC: Department of the Army (15 December 2006)

_____. Field Manual 100-23 Peace Operations. Washington, DC: Headquarters, Department of the Army (December 1994).

U.S. Department of Defense, Joint Publication 3-24, Counterinsurgency Operations. 5 October 2009.

U.S. Department of State. FY 2012 Mission Strategic Resource Plan: U.S. Mission to Mexico (2010). Internal document, not specifically cited in this paper.

_____. U.S. Government Counterinsurgency Guide (January 2009). http://www.state.gov/documents/organization/119629.pdf

United States Senate Caucus on International Narcotics Control. "U.S. and Mexican Responses to Mexican Drug Trafficking Organizations." United States Senate (May 2011).

Villiers Negroponte, Diana. "Mexico Denies 'Insurgency': Implications for an Appropriate Response." Brookings Institution (27 October 2010). http://www.brookings.edu/opinions/2011/0214_mexico_negroponte.aspx

Waghelstein, John, and Donald Chisholm. "Analyzing Insurgency." Newport, RI: Naval War College, 2006.

Winnefeld, ADM James A., Jr. "Statement Before the House Armed Services Committee." Congressional Record (30 MAR 2011).

www.ingramcontent.com/pod-product-compliance
Lightning Source LLC
Chambersburg PA
CBHW052030280526
45793CB00005B/1190